I CRY TO YOU,
O LORD!

SCRIPTURAL

REFLECTIONS

on the MYSTERY

and MEANING

of SUFFERING

D1502969

I CRY TO YOU,
O LORD!

SCRIPTURAL REFLECTIONS *on the* MYSTERY *and* MEANING *of* SUFFERING

FR. JUDE WINKLER, OFM CONV

the WORD among us® Press

Published by The Word Among Us Press
9639 Doctor Perry Road
Ijamsville, Maryland 21754
www.wordamongus.org

12 11 10 09 08   1 2 3 4 5

ISBN: 978-1-59325-115-4

Cover design by The DesignWorks Group

Made and printed in the United States of America

Library of Congress Cataloging-in-Publication Data

Winkler, Jude.
  I cry to you, O Lord! : scriptural reflections on the mystery and meaning of
suffering / Jude Winkler.
     p. cm.
  ISBN 978-1-59325-115-4 (alk. paper)
  1. Suffering--Biblical teaching. I. Title.
  BS680.S854W56 2008
  248.8'6--dc22

                                    2008023223

To my brother Gilbert, who has taught me
the true meaning of courage and faith in the way
he has lived this mystery in his life.

Out of the depths I cry to you, O Lord.
Lord, hear my voice!

—Psalm 130:1-2

TABLE OF CONTENTS

WHAT IS A MYSTERY?

When we hear the word "mystery," we most often think of a book or a TV program that presents a crime story. By the end of the work, we fully expect to find out "who did it." The better the mystery, the more twists and turns we have to navigate in order to arrive at the conclusion, but there is always a conclusion.

We cannot say the same thing about theological mysteries. In theology, mysteries are not problems to be solved; they are ideas that go so far beyond our understanding that we will never fully comprehend them. One responds to theological mysteries with awe. One deals with theological mysteries not with science but with faith. We believe, even when we cannot fully understand.

People often ask how we can believe what we cannot fully comprehend. However, there are many mysteries in life that we never fully comprehend. We have probably never seen a virus. We have seen pictures of what scientists tell us are viruses, but we have little proof that the pictures were not fabricated. How can we believe that what they depict are viruses? And yet, we do believe. We get our flu shots to protect us from those viruses, even if we don't fully understand what they are or how they work. We don't fully understand gravity either, or how it works. Yet, we do believe that it exists.

Even love can be put into this category of mystery. None of us can measure love. We have a sense of when it is strong or in trouble, but we can't say that we have "a liter" or "a pound" of love. And still, we believe that it exists. We even base our lives upon that fact.

Thus, mysteries do not need to be figured out to be significant in our lives. Of course, that doesn't mean that we can't know anything about them. We are supposed to reflect upon theological mysteries. We pray and we study. We especially consider what God has revealed, for some of the mysteries in theology, such as the Trinity, would never be known if God had not revealed them to us.

When St. Augustine wrote about the mystery of God, he used the analogy of water in the ocean. We can never get to know *all* of the water in the ocean, but we can swim around and know what that water is like around us.

There is another story about St. Augustine that illustrates this point. One day, he was walking along the beach and reflecting upon the mystery of the holy Trinity when he came upon a young boy who was playing in the sand. The boy had dug a hole, and he was carrying bucket after bucket of water from the sea and emptying them one after another into the hole. After watching him for a while, St. Augustine asked the boy what he was doing. The boy answered, "I am emptying the ocean into this hole." St. Augustine responded, "You'll never empty the whole ocean in that hole." The child retorted, "I'll empty the ocean in this hole long before you figure out the mystery of the Trinity."

And so, we approach mysteries with awe, respect, and humility. There are things that are, and always will be, beyond our understanding. This is especially true of a mystery as profound as that of suffering. We are not going to figure out exactly why there is suffering or why certain people suffer more than others. We will not be able to understand why so many innocent people in the world suffer so much. When we finish this reflection on the mystery of suffering, there will probably be many more questions than when we began.

So why even begin to reflect upon it? We reflect upon this mystery so that we can swim around in it a bit and know more about the water in which we are swimming. Besides, there is no escaping it. All of us experience a share of suffering, and some of us seem to experience more than our fair share. We have to deal with it. We have to ask why a good God would let us undergo these trials. We have to struggle with our own suffering, and what is often even more difficult, with the suffering of those whom we love. We have to try to make some sense of it.

SUFFERING IS MESSY

One of the biggest difficulties is that most forms of suffering are messy. When we read the stories of the great saints, especially the martyrs, it can sound so glorious. But suffering is far from glorious.

If our suffering is physical, it might be a form of suffering that is embarrassing. It might be something that we are afraid to admit to others. Or maybe we look good on the outside while we are in physical agony on the inside.

Or the suffering might be emotional. We may be in the midst of a relationship with someone whom we are trying to love but who makes it very difficult for us. Or we may have a child or a parent or a sibling who is mentally ill, and we hurt for their pain and for the ways that others misunderstand them.

We may be depressed and feel as if we can't even pray, and worst of all, we may feel guilty about it. This is one of the cruel ironies of depression—that we not only feel awful but that we also feel guilty for feeling that way.

Our suffering might be more subtle. It may be that we have to give up some of our dreams and admit that the things we had hoped would happen in our lives are just not going to happen. It can be so difficult to give up on our hopes and dreams. At times we have to permit ourselves a good cry over what is or what is not, let go of our grief, and then move on.

There is the horrible loneliness we face when we have to say good-bye to those whom we love as they go to the Lord.

Or our suffering might involve the feelings of diminishment we experience as we grow older. We don't have the energy that we once did. We have to give up certain activities. We may have to sell the house where we raised our family, where we have been living for many years, and that's heartbreaking. We may have to let others take over some of our responsibilities, possibly things that we have handled for decades. It can be so very difficult to watch others do things differently than the way we did them and still want them done.

We may also have to say good-bye to other places that are dear to our hearts, such as our parish church. Maybe the church that we have prayed in since we were very young is closing.

How Do We Respond to Suffering?

What happens when the suffering we experience overwhelms us, and we hit a wall? We can't go forward, we can't go back, and we can't go around it. At that point, although we don't have a choice about ending the suffering, we do have a choice about how we will respond to it. We can become angry and cynical and frustrated, or we can surrender and find peace.

As we survey the Old and New Testaments, we will examine how those in Scripture choose to respond to their suffering. Then we will talk about the value of suffering, and the choice we have of how to respond to it—by placing ourselves in God's hands.

This doesn't mean that God will make it all better. God doesn't always make it all better, but God does make all the difference. If I know in the deepest part of my heart that God is there for me and that God will always be there for me no matter what happens, then I can trust. I can find the strength to say, "Not my will, but your will be done."

And yet, we will never "figure it out." As we reflect on suffering in the Old and New Testaments, we may get an insight that will help us to make a little sense of it. Maybe we will see the fuzzy outlines of understanding just before they fade back into the midst. Maybe we will reach the point that Job did, and we will be able to say, "Now I understand that I don't really understand, and so I can only trust."

PART ONE

SUFFERING IN THE SCRIPTURES

Chapter 1

Suffering and Sin: Genesis and Wisdom Literature

The people of Israel firmly believed that the God of all eternity revealed himself in and through their history. The account of this revelation is found in the Old Testament. The Old Testament was written over a period of some twelve hundred years, and it was written by many different authors. Some books, in fact, were the product of hundreds of years of contributions from various schools of literature. They were also written in various literary styles, such as history, prophecy, or wisdom literature. Some of these books are more symbolic and others are more straightforward presentations.

It is important to remember that the people of Israel grew in understanding of God's revelation over time. In earlier days, they believed that Yahweh was their God, but that other gods existed for the other nations (this is called henotheism). Only around the ninth century B.C. did they clearly adopt monotheism, the belief that only one God exists. In earlier days, they often spoke of corporate responsibility for sin. If the king sinned, the nation sinned, or if a parent sinned, the children inherited that sin. Around the time of the Babylonian exile in 587 B.C., the prophets began to speak of individual responsibility for sin.

Even a belief as fundamental as life after death was slow to develop. In the earlier days of Israel's history, people believed in Sheol, a shadowy place where all people went when they died. Only after the exile did they begin to speak of the resurrection of the dead.

Thus, it should be no surprise that there are various responses to the mystery of suffering in the Old Testament. Some of the differences are because of different viewpoints taken over time. Others come from various schools of thought that existed at the same time that took different approaches to the same question. Each viewpoint has something to offer, but each also shows certain weaknesses that must be addressed. Great mysteries of our faith are often so profound that no one viewpoint can tell the whole truth, and that is certainly true of the Old Testament's understanding of the mystery of suffering.

THE VIEW OF SUFFERING IN THE ANCIENT WORLD

Before we reflect on what the Hebrews thought about suffering, let's take a step backward and look at how suffering was viewed in the ancient world. For thousands of years, people have reflected upon suffering and why it happens. Sages and priests of ancient times had various suggestions concerning why we suffer.

One theory was that it was simply our fate to suffer. People believed that history went along in a cyclical pattern that continuously repeated itself. If you happened to be unfortunate enough to be around when a time of suffering occurred, then you suffered. There was no rhyme or reason to it—it just happened.

Another theory was that suffering occurred as a punishment for something you did. The gods had been offended, so they punished us. The greatest difficulty in this ancient concept was that people often did not even know what offended the gods, so they lived in a constant state of terror. Fearing that whatever they said or did might be offensive, they were constantly making offerings to "buy back" the favor of the gods.

At other times, suffering was seen as caused by the actions of incredibly capricious gods. Plagues, wars, and natural disasters, such as the ancient Babylonian flood story, were all viewed as attempts by the gods to silence humans. Men and women had been created to be the slaves of the gods. Now, since they had multiplied, they were making too much noise, keeping the gods up at night. The Greek gods were viewed in a similar way—they were often considered to be mean and capricious, playing with humans for their selfish amusement.

Another ancient theory is that suffering is the result of a collision of opposite forces. In this theory's most ancient form, the gods of order clashed with the gods of chaos. The chaos gods were constantly trying to destroy the order of creation, to return it to its primitive state where everything was formless and void. Two of these gods, in fact, went by the Hebrew names Leviathan and Behemoth.

A later version of this "eternal combat" theory was that there was a good god and a bad god who were constantly battling each other. The good god could be said to be winning when everything was going well, while the bad god was said to be winning when there was war or disease or natural disasters like earthquakes. The Persian form of this belief was called Zoroastrianism, a religion that still exists in the Middle East and India.

Still one other ancient idea was that suffering was the way that we learn to be patient. We suffer to learn. This was the belief of the Stoics. They also argued that we suffered most when we allowed ourselves to become too involved with the affairs of this world. This world is material and, according to the Stoics, corrupt. They taught that our goal in life is to reject the material in order to become more spiritual. The more we are indifferent to what is going on around us, the less the turmoil of life will affect us. This is why we still call someone who seems to be detached from the struggles of life a "stoic."

In the modern view, of course, all of these ideas fall short. We don't believe that blind fate determines our course; we don't believe in many gods who are fighting for control of the universe; we don't believe in a God who would punish us for unintentional transgressions. The Hebrews also had problems with such views. They believed that there was only one God, that he controlled all things, that he was good, and that he was both just and merciful.

The Book of Genesis

The first time that the Hebrew people speak of sin and suffering is in the Book of Genesis. God created Adam and Eve and had a special relationship with them. He cared for them, placing them in the garden of Eden. He gave them free rein of the garden, telling them that they could eat the fruit of any of the trees in the garden with the exception of the tree in the middle—the tree of the knowledge of good and evil. In Hebrew symbolism, when one speaks of the two extremes, one is also speaking about everything in between them. Thus, the tree of the knowledge of good and evil is actually the tree of all knowledge. (There is a second tree in the story, the tree of life, to which Adam and Eve lose access when they sin.)

Of course, what did Adam and Eve do as soon as they had a chance? They ate some of the fruit from the forbidden tree. (Traditionally we say that this was an apple, but this is only because the words for "evil" and "apple" in Latin are so similar. The old saying is that the sin had nothing to do with the apple in the tree; it was about the pair on the ground!)

Soon after Adam and Eve sinned, they heard God walking in the garden in the cool of the evening. On previous occasions, they would accompany God on his walk. That evening, after they had sinned, they recognized their guilt and nakedness and were ashamed, so they hid themselves from God.

What a tragedy! God was the one who loved them. He loved them more than they loved themselves. Even after they had sinned, God continued to love Adam and Eve. But because of their sin, a rift developed, not only between God and Adam and Eve, but also between God and their descendents.

There was also a rift between Adam and Eve. They had been created for each other. Yet, when God asked Adam why he had sinned, he turned on Eve and blamed her. He even blamed God for having given her to him. Adam should have protected his wife, and instead he pushed her into the firing line. Likewise, Eve was created to be Adam's most intimate companion, and instead she tempted him to sin. These facts show that sin had created a rift among human beings.

There was even a rift between humans and nature. When God asked Eve why she did this horrible thing, she answered that the snake had made her do it.

So the first punishment that Adam and Eve suffered for their sin was this triple alienation—from God, from one another, and from nature. This alienation was healed only when Jesus died on the cross.

The curse of alienation, however, was not the only punishment for their sin. In chapter 3 of Genesis, we hear about three other punishments imposed upon Adam and Eve and the snake.

God tells Adam that he will work in the fields but never receive a proper recompense for the difficult work that he does (Genesis 3:19). Notice that work itself is not a punishment for sin. God and Adam worked in the garden of Eden even before Adam and Eve had sinned. The punishment upon Adam was that the work would be frustrating.

Eve received a double punishment. She would suffer terrible pain when she gave birth to her children. What should have been a joyous occasion was accompanied by horrific pain. Furthermore, the woman would desire her man, but he would lord it over her (Genesis 3:16). Notice that God did not intend women to be subordinate to men. The subordination was a punishment, not the original order. One could easily conclude that this particular punishment should be considered to be abrogated now that Jesus has healed the wounds of our sin upon the cross.

We also hear that the snake would lose its legs and would have to lick dust all the days of its life (Genesis 3:14). The snake would be in a constant battle with humanity (3:15), with the snake bruising the heel of Adam's and Eve's descendant, who would in turn bruise its head. In the original Hebrew, the descendant is male, thus referring to King David, who crushed the Moabites. The Moabites worshipped their god in the form of a snake. The early Christians saw this descendent as Jesus, who crushed the power of Satan upon the cross. In the Greek translation of this text, the pronoun is in the feminine, thus referring to Mary.

The Moment Suffering Entered the World

Many have interpreted this third chapter of Genesis as being the moment when suffering entered the world, as a punishment for sin. According to this view, before then, Adam and Eve lived in a utopian state in which there was no suffering. In fact, later in Genesis we hear that all creatures were vegetarians until sin grew more powerful in the world and animals began to eat one another (9:3-6). We have to ask ourselves, though, whether it is proper to understand this text as the moment when suffering entered the world.

Scripture must always be read in light of its literary style. Parables must be understood to be parables, poetry as poetry, and history as history. What is the literary style of this chapter (and, in fact, of the rest of the first eleven chapters of the Book of Genesis)? This chapter is an *etiology*.

Etiologies are stories that explain the origin of some object or event. They are more like parables than scientific explanations. Many cultures, for example, have an etiology concerning the origin of the rainbow—that it is a bow that one of the gods hung in the heavens (and lightning would be the arrows that this god shot from that bow).

We sometimes use etiologies in everyday life when we try to explain a complex idea to a child. If that child asks what thunder is, we probably would not say, "It is caused by electrostatic charges that are released into the atmosphere, causing air molecules to expand and contract at a rapid rate, which creates a massive sound wave." We might instead tell the child that the angels had decided to redecorate in heaven, and the sounds of the thunder were the angels moving their furniture. We know that this is not the scientific explanation, but it is the best that the child could understand.

Likewise, the stories in the first eleven chapters of Genesis are told at a symbolic level to explain what happened in the early days of creation. There is a profound truth in these stories: that

God created everything, that all that he created was good, that he created humans in his image and likeness, that we rejected God's love through sin. But they are not, and never were intended, to be understood as scientific explanations.

The punishments in chapter 3 of Genesis explain why humans have to struggle so much in life, and why no matter how much we try, we can't seem to get ahead. They explain why women suffer childbirth pains. They explain why women would still seek the companionship of men, even when they lord it over them. Finally, they explain why snakes do not have legs and why they have to move from place to place in such a strange manner.

These were things that just did not make sense unless they were a punishment for something. And so the author of this chapter describes the origin of these things in terms of a series of punishments.

Furthermore, the punishments described here were not intended to be an explanation for all suffering in the world. They were explanations only for the things that they mention: the frustration of work, childbirth pains, and legless snakes.

WISDOM LITERATURE

Wisdom literature began as a series of instructions on how to live the good life. Originally, it was probably intended for the sons of the royal family so they could learn how to rule the nation. Eventually, wisdom literature was applied to the lives of all believers. This is what we see in the Book of Wisdom. It says that God did not intend for us to die (or suffer), but that the first sin brought death into the world. We see the connection between suffering and death in the wisdom psalms as well.

What was the formula for a good life? It was observance of the law. God had given Israel the gift of the law so that his chosen people would know exactly what was expected of them. If they observed the law, they would be rewarded with a long, healthy, and happy life. Those who did not follow the law would be punished.

Furthermore, throughout most of Israel's history, the reward or punishment was believed to occur in this life. The reason was that the Jewish people did not believe in the afterlife until relatively late in their history. Before they developed this belief, they taught that all people went to Sheol when they died. Sheol was a place of shadows—you were not really alive and had no emotion or memory. You could not even pray when you were in Sheol.

You were simply there. Thus, your reward had to come in this life. The wisdom psalms promised that this would be the case.

Given this formula, you would have to conclude that any suffering you endured must be a punishment for sin. In the early days of Judaism, that could include being punished for the sins of one's ancestors. Later in the history of Israel, the prophets spoke about individual responsibility for sin. This is what Ezekiel meant when he said that God was setting aside the old proverb, "The parents have eaten sour grapes, and the children's teeth are set on edge" (Ezekiel 18:2). According to that view, you were not punished for what others did, whether it be your parents or the king; you suffered for your own sins. "It is only the person who sins that shall die" (18:4).

This idea—that you suffered for your own sins—was certainly a positive development in the theology of Israel. But there was also a downside. If you were suffering, it must mean that you had done something to deserve that suffering. You must have sinned.

Doubts in the Theory

At a certain level, the theory that sin and suffering are intimately connected makes sense. We only have to consider the troubled spots of the world to see how sin can cause suffering. Furthermore, if you live a sinful life, it will most probably have an impact on your health as well as on your relationships. Yet, can anyone really say that all suffering is an inevitable consequence of sin? Don't the innocent suffer? Don't some good people die early and miserably, while some evil people live long, successful lives? Something seems to be wrong with the theory.

Some of the Old Testament authors recognized the difficulties in connecting sin with suffering. In Psalm 73, the psalmist is scandalized by the fact that those who reject God's law are fabulously successful, while he carefully observes God's law and is not very successful. He spends a number of verses speaking of the charmed lives of the wicked, and you can almost hear the contempt in his voice (Psalm 73:4-12). He is shockingly honest, all but indicting God for what he considers to be a violation of the Lord's promises.

At a certain point, however, the psalmist buckles. He speaks of going to the temple and realizing that God will suddenly bring down his judgment upon the earth (verses 18-20). Those who are evil will be punished severely, while those who are good will be rewarded. From the psalmist's point of view, God is not really ignoring what's going on; he is only waiting for the right moment to strike.

This conclusion is a bit disappointing, for it sounds almost as if the psalmist had realized how far out on a limb he had crawled, and he became frightened and scampered back to the standard wisdom teaching. He accuses himself of having had confused thoughts, and in verse 22, of having been little better than an animal—"I was like a brute beast toward you." In effect, he says that his accusations were all his mistake, thus absolving God of any guilt.

There is one phrase in the psalm that is interesting, for it seems to go beyond the theology of the day. The psalmist speaks of how God will receive him at the end. Remember, Jewish people originally believed that everyone—good, bad, or indifferent—went to Sheol. Here, the psalmist is suggesting that Sheol would not be his ultimate fate. He was going to be with God when he died. (This and Psalm 49 are the only two psalms that speak of the afterlife.)

In spite of the fact that the psalmist finished his presentation by returning to the standard wisdom teaching, by mentioning the afterlife he was opening up new possibilities in this whole question. Belief in the afterlife allowed for the possibility that even if you suffered here and now, if you remained righteous, then you would eventually be rewarded for your patience. This meant that you could no longer judge things by what you saw—how long you lived, whether you were successful—because there was a reality that lay beyond this world.

The question of suffering is also addressed in the book of the prophet Habakkuk. Like Psalm 73, the prophet observes that life does not seem to be fair. Why doesn't God intervene and punish the arrogant? The answer given is that God will use a people he had chosen, the Babylonians, to punish the wicked. The prophet objects that the Babylonians themselves will become arrogant, but the response is that they will also be punished in due time. Anyone who is greedy, who steals what belongs to others, who builds their treasure upon the suffering and death of others, will be punished. Again, the prophet is not saying that the wisdom theory is wrong, only that one has to have patience until it works itself out.

All these answers to the question of suffering are obviously unsatisfactory. It does not seem that all suffering came from the first sin or even from subsequent sins. It does not seem that good people always fare better in life than evil people. Even the Book of Job, a book about suffering, provides no explanation for it.

A Good God

Would a good God bring suffering upon his children? Many people find this idea offensive because it makes God appear to be nasty and vindictive. For many, it recalls the portrait of an angry God found in many texts in the Old Testament.

First of all, that portrait of an angry God is a bit deceptive. The Jewish people wrote the Old Testament through the inspiration of the Holy Spirit, but they also put some of their own concepts and understandings into the text. This is why we needed Jesus to come along—to explain to us who God really is.

Furthermore, the picture of God in the Old Testament is not universally angry. There are many passages that display a warmth and intimacy that serve as the basis of many of Jesus' claims about God in the New Testament.

There might also be something going on here in the so-called "angry" passages. The message that God was trying to communicate might have been understood in a confused manner. God loves us and wants what is good for us. When we sin, we bring spiritual death into our lives. In a sense, we strangle the Spirit, the breath of God within us. God is like a parent who sees a child doing something that is self-destructive and dangerous, much like a parent who sees a child taking drugs. God worries for the child, but is enraged at the drugs that are killing the beloved child. God loves us but hates the sin that is slowly killing us. Might God be angry when we sin? Of course God is angry, but not *at* us. God is angry *for* us.

A God who would call his son Jesus to die on the cross for us certainly has plans that we find mysterious. St. Paul speaks of the wisdom of the cross that goes beyond our own human way of thinking and that some would consider to be folly or a stumbling block. Let's see how suffering is viewed in the Book of Job. Then we will turn to the New Testament to see what its authors have to say about suffering in light of the cross and resurrection of Jesus.

Chapter 2

Honesty and Surrender: The Book of Job

The belief in the wisdom literature, that we suffer as punishment for our sins, is certainly what we find in the Book of Job. However, we also find a man who is willing to express his anger, confusion, and frustration to God. In the end, he doesn't understand the mystery of suffering anymore than in the beginning, but he does decide to surrender to the majesty of God.

This book was written sometime around 450 B.C., after the return of the Jews from exile in Babylon. It tells the story of a heroic figure named Job. This is most probably a fictional account. The author names his protagonist Job, for that is the name of one of the great heroes of the past (like the name Daniel).

Job is a good and righteous man who is wealthy and happy. This is just as it should be, according to wisdom literature. One day Satan spots him and decides to make some trouble. He challenges God: is Job really praising him because he is a righteous man or because he is rewarded for being righteous? Notice that this question addresses one of the flaws that we encounter in wisdom literature—that the only motivation for goodness might be the reward that a person expects from God. It's almost as if a person's good actions are a type of bribe paid to God to receive riches. Satan is questioning whether Job's righteousness springs from his heart and is truly sincere, or whether it is simply a selfish ploy. Of course, this same question could at times be asked of us. Are we being good because at the core of our being we love God, or are we doing it to earn an eternal reward?

Before we go on, we have to ask what Satan is doing in heaven. In the Old Testament, Satan was considered to be part of God's heavenly court. He was a type of district attorney who traveled throughout the earth and then reported back to God what he had discovered. This is why the Book of Revelation calls Satan "the accuser of our comrades . . . who accuses them day and night before our God (Revelation 12:10).

Before we arrive at the pearly gates, Satan will accuse us of all the sins we have committed throughout our life. If God were to judge us with strict justice, then all of us would be condemned to hell. But God sent his Son to die for us. He shows us mercy and offers us forgiveness. (This does not mean, however, that everyone will automatically go to heaven, for some might very well reject that mercy and love and choose to be their own god, which is what hell is all about.) Note that the one who demands strict justice is not God; it is Satan. The next time that we demand strict justice upon others, we might very well ask ourselves whether we are acting more like God or Satan.

Satan asks God to take back all of the blessings that he had given Job. God allows Satan to do this. At first, he permits Satan to take back material possessions and harm Job's family, but he does not allow Satan to harm Job physically. Eventually, though, God even lets Satan torment Job with horrific physical suffering. Job is left scraping sores off his body ißn an ash heap.

The way that this passage is phrased in the first and second chapters makes it seem as if Satan were the actual agent of these disasters while God sits back and allows it to happen. Does that mean that Satan is the author of bad things and that God allows but does not cause suffering? While one might reach this conclusion based on the first few chapters of the Book of Job, the rest of the book makes it clear that Job does not accept that logic. He repeatedly accuses God of bringing disaster down upon him. He does not let God off the hook.

THE "IMPATIENCE" OF JOB

So God allows Satan to bring suffering into Job's life. Job loses his flocks and herds. His possessions are all stolen or destroyed. He even loses his beloved children, for whom he had shown such great love and care. Job accepts his fate, saying that he came forth from his mother's womb naked and that he will go back to that womb in the same way—the "womb" being the earth (1:21). Adam, the first man, was formed from the dirt of the earth, so the earth is, in a sense, the mother of all human beings.

Eventually, Job is left desolate and miserable. Yet he refuses to reject God because of his calamities. His wife encourages him to curse God so that he might die and end his misery. Remember that at this time and throughout most of the Old Testament period, people did not really believe in an afterlife with rewards or punishments. When one died, one went to Sheol, where there would be no more suffering. Yet Job refuses to curse God. His reasoning is that if we bless God for good things, then we should also bless God when bad things happen.

At this point, three of Job's friends, Eliphaz, Bildad, and Zophar, arrive to console him. Their first reaction, however, is not to reach out to him with consoling words. When they see him and how horribly he is suffering, they are reduced to a stunned silence. They cannot say a thing to him for the next seven days.

When Job's three friends regain their ability to speak, they each begin a series of dialogues with Job. It is in these dialogues that we discover what is going on in Job's heart. We have a saying, "the patience of Job." Well, he is patient—for two chapters. Then we have thirty chapters of complaining and anger and expressions of betrayal.

At first Job does not blame God for his difficulties. He just wishes it would end. He curses the fact that he was ever born (3:3). He begs for the shadows of Sheol to come upon him, for at least then he would not have to suffer anymore. People usually begged God to deliver them from going down into Sheol. Job is actually asking to die so that the torment would be over.

Was Job's request to die acceptable to God? People often pray to die when they are being tormented by horrendous physical or emotional suffering. If we want to die because we feel that it is our time to go to the Father, and we want to be with God and with our loved ones who have preceded us, then we can by all means pray for death, either for ourselves or our loved ones. However, some people pray to die because they are running away from life and rejecting it. The distinction can often be fuzzy: when people pray for death, are they rejecting life, or are they just asking for some relief from the cross that they are carrying?

JOB'S THREE FRIENDS ABUSE HIM

Job's three friends had come to offer him comfort, but their role quickly changes. They wanted to help him, and they believed that the best thing that they could do was to offer him their most considered advice. Job was suffering, and according to the wisdom tradition, that meant that he must have done something bad to deserve his suffering. God is, after all, just. God would never allow someone to suffer if that person did not deserve it. So Job must have sinned. The three friends tell Job that all he has to do is admit that it is all his fault, and God will surely relent and take back his punishment.

While Job is a righteous and pious man, he cannot agree with his friends. He knows that he is a sinner, just like the rest of us. But he argues with his friends that he has not done anything serious enough to deserve the misery that he is enduring (see chapter 6). Something is wrong, and he wants God to explain what is going on.

Job's friends are horrified by his reasoning (see chapter 8). By saying that he is not at fault, Job is saying that someone else is at fault, and the only other person whom someone could blame is God himself. They argue that Job is calling God unjust and a liar (since Job is accusing God of failing to fulfill his promises). Thus, they argue, Job is doubly guilty. He is guilty, first of all, for whatever he had done to deserve his trials, and then he is guilty of not accepting his fate with humility and bowing to God's will.

Job becomes frustrated with this reasoning. The three friends are arguing from what they know to be the wisdom of old, but Job is expressing what he knows to be true, for it is coming from his heart. Job tells his "friends" that they are false friends (see chapter 13). He tells them that they should have remained silent, as they had been on the first days they visited him, instead of tormenting him with their worthless theories.

This episode is a warning to us when we want to offer consolation to those who are suffering. We often want to find the perfect words to ease their pain. The danger is that, all too often, our words sound like pious platitudes instead of a sincere attempt to enter into the sufferings of the other. At times, it is better to hold someone's hand and let a tear run down our cheek than to say something that could sound cheap.

JOB CHALLENGES GOD

Job and his three friends become increasingly frustrated with each other. They attack each other's character, both openly and subtly. Eventually, though, Job realizes that his fight is not really with his friends. They are only mouthing theories that were intended to defend the reputation of God. Job therefore realizes that he has to address his real opponent: God.

Even as he says it, Job knows that one cannot win in a fight against God. We are creatures; God is the Creator. Our knowledge and power are sorely limited; God's are not. Therefore God will win every fight. Job still challenges him to appear and fight it out. Job taunts God in the hope that he might appear and explain himself. He says that he wishes he had a chisel so that he could write his complaints against God on the wall, so that anyone who ever passed by could read how shabbily God had treated him (19:24). He even says that he feels like a dried-up leaf that God is blowing around the courtyard to amuse himself (13:25).

As Job rants on, he alludes to some of the most frequently used concepts and images of the Old Testament, but he turns them on their head. Sheol was considered to be a place so unpleasant for its nothingness that one would beseech God to deliver one from going there. Job begs to be able to die and hide in Sheol. In the Old Testament, people often begged God to look down upon their difficulties and intervene. Job asks for the opposite, begging God to look away and forget him. If this is what happens when God is looking at him, then maybe it would be better if God just looked the other way—Job cannot afford for God to pay more attention to him! In the Old Testament, glory and honor are usually associated with God. In Psalm 8, the psalmist asks God why he makes so much of man, crowning him with glory and honor (8:5), meaning that humans are truly created in God's image and likeness. Job turns this idea around and asks God why he makes so much of man. Why does God spend all of his time figuring out how he could make Job's life more miserable?

By the end of his complaint, Job has effectively accused God of being no better than a capricious, sadistic child—one who would torment bugs for his amusement. One would think that such an accusation would provoke God to send a lightning bolt from the heavens to punish Job for his insolence, but that is not what happens. At the end of the story, God congratulates Job for being honest with him while he accuses Job's friends of mouthing pious platitudes that they do not really understand.

Expressing Our Anger to God

Does this mean that God is giving us the green light to express our anger toward him? Anger is usually not a choice; it is an emotion. If we feel something strongly but suppress it, then the emotion tends to come out in another, usually ugly, way. It is like overpacking a suitcase, having to sit on it in order to close its latches. What is bound to happen to the suitcase? Inevitably, the latches break open in public and our underwear flies out for everyone to see. It is much better to take a sweater out of the suitcase and wear it so that the suitcase will close and stay closed. In other words, we should not suppress emotions, but instead find healthy ways to express them.

When we are angry at God, we should tell him. Prayer is supposed to be an honest dialogue with God. If we only tell

God what we think he wants to hear, we are effectively lying to him. Furthermore, it is a sign of distrust when we are not honest with God, for it is like saying that we don't trust him enough to forgive us our outbursts. God is big; God can take it. Besides, if we don't express our anger or disappointment or confusion or frustration, then these feelings will tend to come out in unhealthy ways, usually being expressed at those whom we love the most and who deserve it the least. (This is not saying that God deserves our anger, but expressing it is sometimes the only way we can get beyond it.)

In all of this, we can learn from the example of Jewish prayers. Jewish people in the Old Testament were very honest in their prayers to God. One of the psalms (30:8-10) can be paraphrased, "God, I am sick. You had better heal me quickly, because if I die, it's going to look bad for you." This is what the Jewish people called *chutzpah*, which we might translate as "nerve." But God seems to like it when people put up a good fight. (Of course, remember that Jacob walks away limping from his fight with God.) We can't win when we fight with God, but we can be honest and true to ourselves in the process. Isn't that a way to "win"? Of course, we don't have to stay angry with God, but it is good to work through it and get to the other side, where we learn how to trust.

One other warning is appropriate here. Many good, religious people think that they have arrived at the "other side" when all they have done is to deny their true feelings. We can usually perceive that they haven't fully worked through it by the fact that their anger comes out in more subtle ways, in the forms of judgmentalism, passive-aggressive tendencies, or depression. Many people are often too frightened to admit what is really lying just below the surface. They might need the help of a good spiritual director or counselor to be able to face their less attractive feelings and deal with them.

Elihu's Argument

The tenor and content of Job's argument eventually silences his three friends. There is nothing left for them to say.

At this point, there is an intervention by a fourth character named Elihu (chapters 32 through 37). This seems to be a later addition made by a scribe who was scandalized with the fact that Job seems to have argued the three friends into silence. We know that Elihu's words are an addition because he is never even mentioned up to this point in the story. Furthermore, his arguments are not really new. They are repetitions of what the three friends had already said, although his words never rise to the literary level of the rest of the book.

It might seem strange to us that a scribe would dare to add these chapters. Isn't that presumptuous, adding one's own thoughts to sacred Scripture? We have to remember that, in the early days, these books were not yet considered to be special. If scribes thought that they could say it in a better way, they would often change it. This is why we often find small changes in the text of the Bible in various manuscripts from ancient times.

Furthermore, couldn't God use situations like this to produce a sacred text? We would have expected a sacred text to be written from beginning to end by the same author, but God works in many mysterious ways. We have to remember this in our own lives. At times we are so convinced that God should appear and work in one way that we miss when God works in another. We don't always meet God on the mountain; we often meet him in the mud and mess of the valley of our everyday lives.

GOD APPEARS

Throughout much of the book, Job had been challenging God to come down and explain himself. At the beginning of chapter 38, God does exactly that. God speaks to Job from the storm. In ancient times, storms were thought of as places where God manifested his power. Lightning was considered to be God's arrows or spears, thunder his voice (see Psalm 29).

God immediately begins to interrogate Job. He asks him whether it was he who laid the world on its foundation. He inquires whether Job knows where the sun is during the night or where the snow is stored during the summer. He asks whether he was the one who placed the stars and constellations in the sky. God asks Job whether he is the one who cares for nature.

Of course, Job must answer that he did not do any of these things, that he is but a creature while God is the Creator. He swallows his pride and bows down to God's wisdom and grandeur, saying, "See, I am of small account; what shall I answer you?" (40:4).

But God continues his interrogation. He speaks of Behemoth and Leviathan, the mythical sea creatures. They were believed to be creatures of chaos, attempting to destroy the boundaries of order that God had established in creation—such as the divisions between lightness and darkness and water and sky. Later in wisdom literature, these horrific creatures are presented as semi-tame dragons that God created as play things, but here the description is more terrifying. The author of the book of Job describes them with particulars taken from two animals that the Jewish people considered to be mysterious and threatening. Behemoth is described in terms taken from the description of the hippopotamus, while Leviathan's description is based upon the description of the crocodile. God asks Job whether he is able to control these creatures. Fundamentally, what God is saying is that for someone who is questioning his motives, Job doesn't know very much.

Once again, Job bows to the inevitable and admits that he was speaking about things that he could not understand. He takes back his accusations and surrenders to the will of God. "I had heard of you by the hearing of the ear, / but now my eye sees you; / therefore I despise myself, and repent in dust and ashes" (42:5-6).

At this point, God passes a judgment upon Job and his three friends. Job is commended for his honesty while the three friends are condemned for their willingness to mouth a position that they did not really believe. They are, in fact, only saved from punishment through the intercession of Job.

The very end of the book is a little disappointing. Job receives back many fold whatever he lost. It's almost as if the author has to conclude with a happy ending. This is disappointing because life doesn't always have a happy ending. We often have to wait for our eternal reward to make sense out of what has happened. But remember, this book was written at a time when most people did not yet believe in an afterlife. There is only a hint of this belief in Job 19:25-27, where Job speaks of seeing God in the flesh, which is probably a reference to the resurrection of the dead. In the rest of the book, Sheol is the fate of all.

So if God is going to work things out, it had to be in this life. This is why the book had to have such a happy ending. There was no other possibility.

So what can be learned from the Book of Job? Certainly, as we have seen, the book admits that suffering can give rise to anger and confusion and frustration. Job is not condemned for having those feelings.

What is surprising, though, is that there is no explanation for why there is suffering. There is only a prescription on how to respond to it. The Book of Job reminds us that suffering is a mystery beyond our understanding, and so we can only eventually surrender to God's will and learn to trust. We can be angry as we seek to make sense of it all, but eventually we must surrender and trust.

CHAPTER 3

Love and Presence:
The New Testament

The revelation of the Old Testament was inspired by the Holy Spirit, but it nevertheless presented God's word in a partial and at times confused manner—not because the word itself was confused, but because the sacred authors were limited in their understanding of the revelation.

This is why it was essential for Jesus to come into the world. He is the full and perfect revelation of who God is and what God wants of us. His story is communicated to us through sacred Scripture and tradition.

The New Testament speaks of this revelation in the gospels, the Acts of the Apostles, the letters, and Revelation. Each of these was written for a particular community with its own individual needs and problems. Jesus' revelation is one, but it is expressed in various ways throughout the New Testament.

Thus, once again, we will find various approaches to the mystery of suffering in the New Testament. This is not because the mystery is peripheral to our faith in Jesus. How could it be when the passion and death of Jesus are so central to our beliefs? We find different approaches because the New Testament was written in various forms of literature and because each of the communities in and for which these books were written had slightly different beliefs (often influenced by how Jewish or Gentile a community was). As we saw when we considered the writings of the Old Testament, each book and each approach has something to offer.

THE GOSPEL OF JOHN

One of the major themes in John's Gospel is based on matrimonial symbolism: that the love of Christ for us, the church, is as intimate and profound as that between a husband and a wife. And it is here that we see a connection between suffering and love.

We see that idea in the story of the miraculous transformation of water into wine at the wedding feast of Cana. Typical of stories of miracles in this gospel, this story is told at two levels. The surface level tells us about a miracle that Jesus performed, changing six jars of water into wine. The second level is the symbolic meaning of the miracle. In fact, this gospel doesn't even call it a miracle. It calls it a sign. A sign is something that points to a greater reality. When we come across a stop sign while driving, we know that we should not stop the car and get out and leave it there. We stop, look, and then go when the way is clear.

The stop sign points us to another level of meaning. Likewise, the signs that Jesus performs point to a greater reality. They call us to faith.

What is the symbolic meaning of the wedding feast of Cana? There is an abundance of wine—too much, in fact. And Jewish people do not believe in getting drunk. There is even a Yiddish saying that a drunk is a Gentile and a Gentile is a drunk. Now, while this saying is a bit insensitive, it nevertheless helps us realize that there is too much wine at the wedding. The reason for is that an abundance of wine is a sign of the heavenly banquet. Jesus was catering not only a wedding feast for the husband and wife but also the heavenly banquet.

When the water made into wine is brought to the steward, he is confused, since the good wine is usually served first. This is "Bartending 101"—first the Beaujolais, then the Muscatel. Jesus did just the opposite. He served the better wine last. The first wine represents the Old Covenant; the second wine represents the New Covenant.

Now, when Mary asked Jesus to do something for the couple, his response was, "Woman, what concern is that to you and to me? My hour has not yet come" (2:4) In English, this sounds terribly insulting, but in Aramaic it simply means, "This is none of our business." What is very interesting is that he says, "My *hour* has not yet come." Jesus' hour in the Gospel of John is his hour of glory, and that is the cross. Usually when we hear the word "glory," we think of power or magnificence. If this were the sense of glory in this gospel, then the "hour of glory" would probably be the resurrection. In this gospel, the word "glory" means the outpouring of love. We see Christ's glory best when we see his love poured out upon the cross. That is his "hour of glory." How is it that we will get to the heavenly banquet? It is through the cross. Jesus is telling his mother that if he helps the couple, then he will end up on the cross.

What is Mary's response? She tells the servants, "Do whatever he tells you" (2:5). This is what Mary always does. She leads people to her Son. Furthermore, by saying this to the servants, she is calling her Son to the cross. She is a parent who loves her child so much that she calls him to sacrifice and love.

In this passage, Mary is playing a symbolic role. Notice that we never really hear Mary's name in this passage. She is consistently called the mother of Jesus. In the Gospel of John, when a character has a title and not a name, that person is playing a symbolic role. This is true of the Samaritan woman at the well (chapter 4), the man born blind (chapter 9), even of the Beloved Disciple (chapter 13). What is the role of the "mother of Jesus"? In the Old Testament, the mother of the king has a significant responsibility: she prepares the wedding feast of her son, the king. This is what Mary does; she calls her Son to the cross.

Called to Generosity and Sacrifice

This is what it means to be a loving parent. The goal of a good parent is not to make one's children happy; it is to call them to be the most that they can be. This might very well mean calling the children to generosity and sacrifice. This may even mean calling one's children to their cross.

A second passage in John's Gospel that connects love and suffering is when Mary, the sister of Martha and Lazarus, anoints the feet of Jesus in chapter 12. She uses a liter of aromatic nard. This was a very costly ointment, worth almost a year's salary. Interestingly, the only place where we hear about this ointment in the Old Testament is in the Song of Songs (1:12). This anointing is a symbol of extravagant love, for when we are in love, we often do extraordinary things. When Judas objects to the extravagance of this gesture, Jesus tells him that she was really preparing him for his burial. Thus, once again, an action of love is associated with an action of suffering.

We see this connection yet again on the cross. In John we read that a soldier had come to break the legs of those who had been crucified (John 19:32-33). This was to hasten their deaths, since they died on the cross by suffocation. When the person was no longer strong enough to push up with his legs to catch his breath, he would die. If his legs were broken, then he would die almost immediately. When the soldier came to Jesus, he found that Jesus was already dead. He went up to him and pierced his side with a lance, and immediately blood and water flowed out (19:34). Blood is a symbol for the Eucharist; water is a symbol for baptism.

This scene reminds us of the account of the creation of the first woman. Jesus on the cross reminds us of when God placed Adam in a deep sleep. Jesus's side was opened, and God opened Adam's side to take out the rib to form Eve. Jesus espouses the church when he dies on the cross, and Adam espoused Eve in the account of her creation.

Now, in Jewish tradition, if a man dies before having a child, then his widow would be expected to marry the next of kin so that she might bear a child who would carry on the name of the deceased. Jesus marries the church on the cross, but he has no children. This is part of the reason why Jesus adopts the Beloved Disciple as his brother. Certainly, he adopts the Beloved to care for his mother, but he also adopts the Beloved to be Jesus' next of kin. He was to marry the church to bear children who would bear Christ's name—Christians. Furthermore, notice that the Beloved Disciple is not named in this account. He must therefore be playing a symbolic role. He stands for all of us, for we are called upon to be Jesus' brothers and sisters, and we are expected to bear children spiritually who bear Christ's name.

And like any truly loving parent, Mary reminds us that the world has run out of wine again. There is so much hurt and hatred in the world, and it desperately needs Christ's love to be manifested once again. This time, however, it is our turn to take up our cross and make Christ's passion and death visible again in our own suffering. This is how we do what the Letter to the Colossians recommends: to make up what is lacking in the suffering of Christ (1:24).

So what could possibly be lacking? Wasn't the suffering and death of God's only begotten Son enough? There is only one thing lacking: to make it present again.

THE BOOK OF REVELATION

For many people, the mysteries of the suffering, death and resurrection of Jesus are nothing more than myths. For many people, Easter has little more meaning than flowers, candles, music, and candy. But the Holy Triduum, the days that run from the evening of Holy Thursday up to the Easter Vigil, are the days that make all the difference in our lives.

How can we help people believe in these sacred mysteries? By living them in our own lives. When we respond to the sufferings in our lives with trust and hope, we become living signs of the paschal mysteries. In fact, the classical definition of a sacrament is a visible sign of an invisible grace. We become sacraments of the passion of Christ. We might be the only form of the cross that people can experience and believe in their lives.

We see a symbolic presentation of this message in the Book of Revelation, chapters 11 to 14. This book is highly symbolic, and that is especially true of these chapters. What at first appears to be a series of unconnected scenes are actually the same story told over and over again. It is like a film that shows a car accident several times in a row, each time viewed from a different angle.

These chapters tell the story of the church that suffers when it gives witness to the Word of God. In 11:1-2, we hear that the visionary is given a measuring stick to measure the inner court of the temple while the outer court is given over to the pagans to trample for forty-two months. For Christians, the body is the temple of the Holy Spirit. The message is that Christians would be persecuted (the outer court that is trampled), but their spirits would be protected (the inner court). In other words, members of the church would be persecuted and even killed, but their spirits would never be harmed. The persecution would last for three and one-half years, the traditional period of time for the tribulation in the Old Testament. But instead of calling it three and one-half years, the author calls it forty-two months. Forty-two months just seems longer than three and one-half years, since when we are suffering, time seems to drag.

The second scene shows two witnesses who will bear witness to their faith. These two witnesses are actually the church, and the witness they give lasts for 1,260 days. Again, this is three and one-half years, but note how much longer 1,260 days seems—even longer than forty-two months, although it is the same amount of time.

In chapter 12, we hear of a woman giving birth to a son who is endangered by Satan. Typical of this book, this scene has two layers of meaning. On one level, the woman giving birth is the Blessed Virgin Mary. She is pictured as standing on the moon and wearing a crown of twelve stars. That, in fact, is the image used to depict the Immaculate Conception. When she gives birth to her Son, the child is endangered by the powers of evil, such as when Herod tried to kill the child Jesus and ordered the murder of all the baby boys in Bethlehem (see Matthew 2:16-18).

But at a second level of meaning, the woman represents the church. She gives birth to the presence of Jesus in the world.

Note, however, that there is an unusual element in this presentation. The child is born and is immediately caught up into the heavens. What is missing here? Jesus' life! We seem to pass from his birth immediately to his ascension. Why? Maybe we are not only talking about Jesus' birth in Bethlehem. Maybe at this second level we are talking about Jesus' birth into glory upon the cross. If that is the case, it would explain the reference to

Satan's activities. He thought he was destroying Jesus by having him crucified, but that was actually the moment when love conquered hate. That was the moment of Christ's exultation.

And so when does the church (the woman) give birth to the presence of Christ in the world? When she re-presents the passion of Jesus in her own suffering. It is then that she becomes a sacrament of the passion of Christ.

This same theme continues in chapter 13, when the forces of evil continually attack those who are faithful to God. These evil forces seem to be winning, but at the beginning of chapter 14, we see this victory is only an illusion. How does good defeat evil? The 144,000 sing a hymn to the Lamb. By doing that, by placing Christ at the center of their hearts, the witnesses have defeated evil.

St. Augustine was once asked, "Does evil exist?" His answer was that it doesn't exist. It is not something that has an independent existence; it is an absence. A vacuum is the absence of air; evil is the absence of good and love. How do we destroy a vacuum? We add air. How do we destroy evil? We add love.

When the church suffers and yet refuses to hate, it destroys the power of hate and evil. By suffering with trust, we destroy the alienation that suffering and sin can cause, just as Jesus destroyed them on the cross. We make the power of the cross, the power of love, present again.

OTHER NEW TESTAMENT TEACHINGS

What else does the New Testament say about suffering? Much of its message is based upon an ancient philosophy called Stoicism. In that philosophy, each person has been given a determined fate. If we surrender to that fate, we find peace. If, however, we oppose that fate, we will suffer. Desire causes suffering, while surrender brings joy.

We find this attitude in the writings of St. Luke and St. Paul. They both proclaim that God has a plan for us (Luke 24:6-7, 25-26, 44; Romans 8:28-30; Ephesians 1:3-6; Galatians 1:15-16). The more that we surrender to that plan, the more we are filled with the Lord's peace. The more we oppose it, the more turmoil we bring into our lives.

St. Paul calls the desires that get us into trouble "passions." We are free in Christ, but freedom doesn't mean that we can do whatever we want. If we only think of ourselves, then we are not really free; we are slaves of our passions. We have to learn to say no to those passions so that we can say yes to Christ (Galatians 5:16-18). That, in itself, can be painful, for most of us want to have our cake and eat it, too. We want everything when we want it and how we want it. Saying no costs us dearly. St. Paul speaks of being crucified to the world (6:14). Even though the world was created as good, sin has confused it so that many of the things that were created good can get us into trouble if we misuse them. So we have to give up even good things to choose what is better: the love of Christ.

Parents know this. They often have to give up even good things so that they can be available to their children. Parents who cannot say no to work or pleasure will sooner or later find that they have not really been present enough for their children. Likewise, parents who crave the approval of their children and cannot bear the pain of being the object of their children's anger will not be able to establish the proper boundaries for their children when it is necessary.

This is the reason why Christians practice fasting and other penitential practices. Food is good, but in our country it is often misused. People eat too much, too little, or the wrong things. Fasting can bring food back into its proper perspective. It can teach us to say no when that is appropriate (both to food and to anything else that might get us into trouble).

Penitential practices can serve as a type of spiritual remedial therapy to strengthen our spiritual muscles. They help us to say no to what is unimportant so that we can say yes to what really counts.

The New Testament also teaches us that suffering can help us to grow in patience and perseverance (Romans 5:3-5; James 1:2-4). When we suffer, we want it to end. When we suffer with hope and trust, we learn to put up with that which is inconvenient and uncomfortable and sometimes even horrific. We learn to view things in terms of eternity (much as God does) and not in terms of what is immediately evident.

In addition, the New Testament teaches that suffering can give us the opportunity to learn from the discipline that God imposes (Hebrews 12:5-13). Discipline sounds like a dirty word to many people today, but we have to remember that it was considered to be one of the most important virtues in the ancient world. God is a loving parent who only wants what is good for his children. Because God loves us, he will at times let us feel the consequences of our poor choices. God does not want us to suffer to get even with us for our offenses. God wants us to grow, and if we have to go through some turmoil to reach that good, God loves us enough to take the risk that we might turn from him in anger and resentment because of what we have gone through.

We could even ask whether God might at times invite us to the cross, not because we have done something wrong, but rather because through the cross we might become more loving people. We might learn how to trust him more. We might experience a more profound compassion for others who are suffering. We might recognize the honor to which God has called us.

The authors of the New Testament could ask, "What did I do to deserve this?" and mean, "Since my suffering is a punishment, what did I do or fail to do?" Instead, they ask, "What did I do to deserve this?" and mean, "Why did God think so highly of me that he invited me to the dignity of the cross?" (see 1 Peter 4:12-14). It is most often on the cross that we are closest to God, for it is then that we realize that we have to hold onto him for dear life lest our lives fall apart. So much else becomes insignificant and unimportant in light of our holding onto God. It is on the cross that we are given the dignity of continuing the saving mission of Christ in our own times.

This is why those who suffer in the New Testament are often filled with a spirit of joy (1 Thessalonians 1:6). They feel that they have been given a great honor, for they are suffering for the gospel. Normally when we suffer, we respond with anger or hurt. When we respond to suffering with joy, it means that we recognize that something very holy is happening. It is a sure sign of the presence of the Holy Spirit.

It is also an opportunity to exercise our priestly dignity, the dignity we received in the Sacrament of Baptism. Like Christ, the High Priest, we are the one making the offering on the altar of our faith, and we are the sacrifice being offered upon the altar. Let us turn, then, to the second part of this reflection, exploring how Jesus responded to suffering so that we can learn how to embrace suffering and trials in our own lives.

Part Two

THE CHRISTIAN RESPONSE TO SUFFERING

CHAPTER 4

BECOMING LIKE JESUS

We've looked at both the Old and New Testaments to see what God has to say about the great mystery of suffering. We still have to accept that suffering is a mystery, but that doesn't mean we have to sit passively as we experience it. As Christians, what should be our response to suffering?

As we look to Jesus, we can see how to respond. We can let suffering bring us down, or we can consecrate it and join our suffering to that of Christ, even as he joined his to ours. As Jesus did, we can suffer with trust and surrender. Through our compassion, we can share in the suffering of others. We can even find joy in suffering.

How does Jesus respond to the suffering he encounters? He does heal lepers and the blind and the lame. But even as he is healing them, he is pointing to the fact that spiritual healing is much more important than physical healing.

For example, after the paralytic was lowered through the roof, Jesus' first words to him were, "Son, your sins are forgiven" (Mark 2:5). As far as Jesus was concerned, this was the more important healing. Jesus may even have preferred to carry this man out of the room, still paralyzed but with a big grin on his face because he knew that Jesus had healed him spiritually. It is only because of the reaction of the Pharisees—they were scandalized that Jesus had said the man's sins were forgiven since only God can forgive sins—that Jesus also heals him physically. He does ask the Pharisees the question, "Which is easier, to say to the paralytic, 'Your sins are forgiven,' or to say, 'Stand up and take your mat and walk'?" (2:9). The answer is that it is easier to heal someone physically. It is easier to heal a broken leg than a broken heart. We have all experienced this truth. When someone hurts us emotionally, it can take years, and even decades, to let go of the hurt.

Another example of this truth is found in the Gospel of John, chapter 9, the story of the man born blind. The disciples ask Jesus whether he is blind because of his sins or because of the sins of his parents. Jesus rejects this standard wisdom teaching. He tells his disciples that the man is blind so that God's works might be made manifest in him (9:3). Again, just picture the man. Jesus has already healed his heart long before he heals his body.

A third example is found in the Gospel of Luke. When Jesus heals someone physically, but there is no expression of faith in the miracle account, Luke uses the word "heal." However when there is an expression of faith during the healing, Luke uses the word "save," meaning that the person is healed both physically and spiritually.

Yes, Jesus came to heal us spiritually. While he was on this earth, he also healed people physically, yet when he ascended into heaven, there were still many ill people in Israel. Why did he heal some people and not others?

This is, in fact, the great scandal of prayer. Why does it seem that some prayers are answered while others are not? Is it that we have not prayed with enough faith? Or might we be using the wrong prayer? Maybe we're praying to St. Thérèse when we should have been praying to St. Anthony. It all sounds as if God were a vending machine. If we put in the right spiritual coin, then out comes our miracle.

But God is not a machine; God is a person. Because God loves us, we have to trust that he will give us the most loving answer to our prayers. Sometimes that answer is that we will be healed physically; other times the Lord tells us that he will meet us on the cross. God does not give us what we want, God gives us what we need. Furthermore, God can see and judge things in terms of eternity. We see in the short term. We see what we think will turn out the best for us, but we can never see all the ramifications of our choices. Maybe what would temporarily be good will turn out to be disastrous in the long run. Our vision is limited; God's is not.

Jesus Joins Us in Our Suffering

Jesus doesn't really explain why there is suffering. More than anything, he joins us in it. He allows himself to be crucified so that when we are on the cross, we will never be alone again.

And when you think about it, isn't that what's most important? When we are suffering, we feel abandoned. We feel as if no one could ever understand what we are going through. Furthermore, we don't feel like imposing our burdens on others because they have enough of their own problems. Jesus joins us in our suffering. He takes on our human condition so that he can be one with us when we suffer.

Jesus also takes up the suffering of our sins on the cross. When we sin, we hurt ourselves. God created us in his image and likeness. He called us to share eternity in his love. By sinning, we are saying to God, to others, and even to ourselves that we are nothing but trash and so we might as well act like trash. When we sin, something dies within our hearts, and we become more like animals than what God created us to be.

God takes that loneliness and hurt upon himself on the cross. He destroys the self-hate by showing us how much he loves us. He loves us to death.

Jesus dies on the cross to reveal how much God has always loved us. God never stopped loving us when we sinned; we turned our back on his love and stopped loving ourselves. Jesus came into the world and told us that he loved us. Our first response was, "What do you want?" This is because many of us have learned to distrust in life. We don't trust other drivers, we don't trust that people will give us the right change, and we don't trust what the telemarketers tell us. It is even difficult to believe when others tell us that they love us, since the word "love" is so often misused today.

So Jesus tells us again that he loves us. At this point, we ask him, "How could you possibly love me when I don't even love myself?" Isn't sin a symptom of how little we think of ourselves? Even when we are forgiven in the Sacrament of Reconciliation, we sometimes cannot let go of the guilt. One of the ironies of growing older is that we can't remember if we took our pills this morning, but we can remember the sins we committed thirty years ago.

We have to remember how much God loves us. A story about the French seventeenth-century saint, Margaret Mary Alacoque, who received the revelations of the Sacred Heart, can help us to realize this truth. Her spiritual director did not believe her visions. So he instructed St. Margaret Mary to ask Jesus in her next vision to reveal to her the sins he had confessed the previous week. The next time she had a revelation, she did ask Jesus, and his response to her was, "I forgot." As God, he can't forget anything, but he was telling her that he had let go of them, and that we should let go of them as well.

Finally, Jesus looks us in the eyes and asks us, "What could I possibly do to prove how much I love you? Would you believe I love you if I were to die for you?" And then he does.

It is important to remember that this is not the only way to speak about how we were redeemed. It is a mystery, and our human words always fall short when we speak about mysteries. But this insight reminds us that God never stopped loving us even when we sinned. We turned our backs on God's love, but God did not stop loving us. Thus the cross is not the moment God changed his mind about us, it is the revelation of what God has always felt about us.

So Jesus took on our suffering, physical and spiritual, so that we will never be alone again. It is in our suffering, in fact, that we are most one with Jesus. When we are suffering, our passion (great suffering) becomes passion (great love).

LEARNING TO TRUST IN THE MIDST OF SUFFERING

We know how difficult it is to respond to suffering with trust in God. Jesus trusted the Father in his agony in the Garden of Gethsemane, even as he prayed to let the cup pass from him. We can also look to the Scriptures to see another example of how to suffer with trust in the story of Abraham and his son, Isaac.

God had made a promise, a covenant to Abraham, to give him a great land and descendants as numerous as the sand on the seashore and the stars in the heavens (Genesis 12: 1-2; 15:5). Yet when Abraham had grown old, he possessed no land, and the only child he had was his son Isaac. (Abraham had another son, Ishmael, but God ordered Abraham to send him away for he was not to be the son of the promise.) Abraham loved Isaac, and he also considered him to be the sign of God's fidelity to his promises.

This is why it was both tragic and a challenge to Abraham's trust in God when God addressed him and told him, "Abraham, take your son, your only son Isaac, whom you love . . . and offer him there as a burnt offering" (Genesis 22:1-2). This must have seemed horrific to him, yet Abraham still obeyed God. He took Isaac and his servants and traveled to the mountain that the Lord indicated to him. He left the servants with the animals while he and the boy climbed up the mountain. Even the details of the climb give an indication of how much he loved the boy. Abraham had Isaac carry the wood for the sacrifice while he carried the fire and the knife. He was not giving his son the heavy burden while he carried the light load; he was giving his son the safer load while he himself carried those objects that might have harmed his son, the fire and the knife.

When they reached the summit, Abraham prepared to sacrifice his son. Before he was able to do it, an angel stopped him and substituted a ram for the sacrifice in place of Isaac.

We can look at this story in hindsight and say that God wasn't going to let Abraham go through with the sacrifice of his son. Even if that is true, however, Abraham didn't know that. As far as he was concerned, his son was all but dead.

Why would God make Abraham do this? Tradition tells us that it was to put Abraham to the test. But God already knows everything. Why did he have to test Abraham? God knows everything, but Abraham did not. Is it possible that Abraham came to understand what unconditional faith and trust meant through this test?

Is it possible that because of how God made us, the only way we can learn what love really means is to be put to the test? Is it through suffering that we learn how to trust when trust does not seem possible? In that case, God is not testing us so that he can give us a final grade; God is testing us so that we can become the most loving people that we can be.

But what if no one knows that we are suffering with trust? What good does it do? There is a level of communication that goes beyond words. It is at the level of love and prayer and faith. When we suffer and yet trust, people can sense it. They might not know what is happening intellectually, but in their hearts they know. And that witness fills them with awe.

Here's one example of such a witness. A ninety-four-year-old sister had suffered a stroke. She could not walk and she could not talk. But when the nurses entered her room in the motherhouse infirmary, she smiled. The nurses encountered an overwhelming sense of peace because they saw that the sister was at peace. They shared that peace with their families, and their families shared it with their neighbors. This sister, whom many in the world considered to be useless, was involved in her most important apostolate: carrying the cross with love. And her witness sent out waves of love that helped transform the world.

One paralyzed sister brings peace to her nurses, who bring that peace to their families, who share it with their neighbors, who share it with their acquaintances. Before one knows it, the world has become a more loving place. One cannot measure it, but it happens. In small, immeasurable ways, each person who trusts in the midst of suffering helps transform the world into the kingdom of God.

COMPASSION: OFFERING TO SUFFER WITH OTHERS

There is a time when we invite suffering into our lives. It is called compassion. The word compassion comes from two Latin words: *cum* and *passio*. "Cum" means "with" and "passio" means "to suffer." When we practice compassion, we offer to suffer with others. We take some of their suffering upon ourselves so that they do not have to carry that burden alone. This is what Jesus did, and this is what he calls us to do for our brothers and sisters in Christ.

Most of us have gone to a funeral home to join in the mourning. Yet, very few of us have raised anyone from the dead. Then what good did we do? The answer is that there is value in just being there. By being present, we made sure that those who lost a loved one would not have to mourn alone. We destroyed the feelings of alienation that people who are suffering often experience. The important thing was not what we said. We often look for the right words, but sometimes just being there, even if we are tongue-tied, is the real value.

A Franciscan friar worked with a group of Iraqi Christian refugees in Rome. He would often visit their homes to talk with them, and at each home he was offered something to drink, whether it was a glass of cold water or a cup of cocoa or Turkish coffee. It was essential for these people to show hospitality, and he had to accept whatever they offered as a sign of respect. One day he visited a family and was offered the requisite cup of Turkish coffee. As he prepared to put a couple of teaspoons of sugar in the cup, his host said to him, "Friar, please do not put sugar in the coffee today. This morning I found out that my father died in Baghdad, and I want you to taste the bitterness of life with me." Drinking that coffee did not make things any better. The host's father was still dead in a far-off land. Yet by sharing the grief and loneliness, it was somehow better.

We practice compassion when we listen to the difficulties of family or friends. Again, we are often tempted to offer what we consider to be words of wisdom that we think will resolve that person's difficulties. But there are times when our advice is unwarranted, because what the person really needs is someone who will listen, not someone who will make it all better. Often when we try to "solve the problem," it reflects more upon our own needs (to have everything ordered, to be in charge, to control the people around us). It takes a lot of patience just to listen and hear and empathize with the person who is venting.

When we do this, we often wish there were something we really could do. But simply by feeling helpless, we have already done some good. We are sharing in the feeling of helplessness

that the other person is experiencing. They are no longer helpless alone, for we are one with them.

SHARING IN OUR PAIN

We could even find an example of compassion in the story of
Abraham and Isaac. We already saw that it represents the testing of Abraham. It was the moment when Abraham learned to
trust more than he thought was ever possible.

But we could easily reread the same story and give it another
level of meaning. (That is what is so wonderful about many of
the stories in the Bible. They can be interpreted at various levels,
which means that they are rich with possible meanings.)

At this second level, we could ask, "Why did God test
Abraham?" The second answer could be stated in terms of compassion. We always like to share our pain with our friends. God
was Abraham's friend. They had a meal together. Abraham could
bargain God down a bit concerning the punishment he intended
to impose upon Sodom and Gomorrah (Genesis 18:20-33).
Abraham was God's friend. And so God shared with Abraham
the pain of losing an only son, a beloved son.

Now it has to be stated that when Jesus died on the cross, God
did not suffer physically. This was a debate that was resolved
in the early days of the church. But did the Father stand by,

indifferent and unbothered, to the plight of his only Son upon the cross? Some philosophers claim that God doesn't have feelings. They believe that any emotion attributed to God is only anthropomorphism—assigning God human traits. They would say that feelings are only signs of inadequacies. (Remember, these philosophers were often either Stoics or influenced by Stoicism, a philosophy that disdained emotion and that counseled its followers to approach life in a "stoical" manner.)

Still, if one reads the Bible, one hears that God loves, hates, rejoices, is angry, and so forth. These are not just anthropomorphisms. These emotional descriptions reveal something of who God is. Of course, ultimately everything we say about God is actually anthropomorphism, because we are using human words to explain a mystery beyond words. But since we only have human words, we must use them.

The Father wanted his Son to die on the cross out of love for us, but this also broke the Father's heart. Yet, he paid the price of love.

So, in the account of Abraham and Isaac, we could also say that he shared that pain with Abraham, letting him know what it was like to lose an only Son (Jesus in the case of the Father, Isaac in the case of Abraham).

We could even take this another step. What does God experience every time we sin? For God, isn't it like losing a beloved child? Isn't this the significance of the image of the Sacred Heart? God sees that our hearts are broken, and God offers us his own heart. And so God lets Abraham feel the pain that he experiences every time that we sin.

There are times when we feel that we are experiencing more suffering than is our fair share. Might it be possible that at those times, we are carrying part of the burden of sin and suffering in the world? Could God be asking us to share in his pain because we are his friends? Might this be part of what it means to continue Christ's work in the world?

Another biblical story that shows compassion is that of Lazarus, the brother of Mary and Martha (John 11). Jesus raises Lazarus from the dead. This is not really a resurrection, it is a re-animation. Resurrection means to receive a new, glorified body that will never die again. Reanimation means that someone is brought back to life, but that person will eventually die again. This is the case with Lazarus, the daughter of Jairus (Luke 8), and the son of the widow of Nain (Luke 7).

We could ask, "What did Lazarus get out of this?" Mary and Martha got their brother back. Jesus got his friend back. The disciples got to see a great miracle and sign. But what did Lazarus get? He was already dead, so he must have been with God. (Even if we say that the he was in the underworld awaiting Jesus' death, within a week he would have been with Jesus

Becoming Like Jesus

in heaven after his death on the cross.) Instead, Jesus brought Lazarus back to life, which meant that he would have to die again. Isn't one death enough? Who would want to have to die twice?

Furthermore, Jesus brought Lazarus back to life one week before Jesus died on the cross. Can't you picture Lazarus standing under the cross and thinking to himself, "I would rather be dead than see this." But maybe this is exactly why Jesus brought him back to life, so that he could share his pain with Lazarus. This is something we do with our friends. Jesus loved Lazarus so much that he wanted Lazarus to be there as he suffered and died. He knew that this experience would make his beloved friend a much more loving person.

There are times in life when we are called to share another's agony. How does it feel, for example, when you realize that you have to put a parent who has dementia in a home, especially if you have cared for that parent for as long as you could? It breaks your heart. But the struggle in making that decision and the pain you feel are forms of compassion. You are sharing in the confusion and fears of that parent, and you are carrying the cross with that parent. Love is doing the best you can, even when no option is all that pleasant. It is easy to choose between good and bad. It is difficult to choose between good and better or bad and worse. The struggle itself can be an act of love, and the torturous doubts can be an act of love. They can be ways of showing love in what seems to be very confused and unloving situations.

The Joy in Suffering

Can we go so far as to say that we may even discover joy in our suffering? There is a story in the Franciscan tradition on this theme. It is called "Perfect Joy" and it is taken from a series of stories called *The Little Flowers of St. Francis*. Although the story is almost certainly fictional, it nevertheless presents the spirit of St. Francis' teachings.

We hear that one day, St. Francis and one of his early companions, Brother Leo, were walking to a church, suffering with cold. Brother Leo asks him what perfect joy would be like. St. Francis says if they arrived at their destination and they knocked at the door and no one answered, and they did not become angry or uncharitable, that would be perfect joy. Or, if one of the porters answered the door and swore at them and then slammed the door in their faces, and they still responded with patience and love, that would be perfect joy. Or, if the porter answered the door again, took a stick and beat them up, leaving them bleeding in the snow, and they still responded with patience and love, that would be perfect joy.

To our modern sensibilities, this story can sound odd. Why would Francis consider these scenarios to be perfect joy?

There are actually two answers. First of all, St. Francis realized that we often love people from mixed motivations. They may be funny, accepting, or easygoing. But what happens when there is absolutely no reason to love a person other than for the love of God? If St. Francis continues to love the brother who insulted and beat him up, then he is loving him for no other reason than for the love of God. He's not going to get anything out of it. He's not going to be welcomed or get a hot meal or a warm bed. In fact, all he'll get is insult and injury. Blessed is he, for now his love is pure.

Jesus taught this truth in the gospels. He spoke about how it is easy to love those who love us. But we are especially called to love those who hate us and to pray for those who persecute us. Then we know that it is true love. We love them because we know that they need it. Ultimately, too, it's not important whether they inherited their brokenness or caused it themselves. Even if they are just suffering the consequences of their own bad choices, the important thing is that we love them.

The second reason why St. Francis is so filled with joy is that by being insulted and beaten, he could now share in the sufferings of Christ, taking that angry man's burdens on himself, as Christ did for us. That is perfect love, which brings us joy.

This does not mean that we have to be a doormat. We don't want to suffer, but if we have anything to do with the people around us, then sooner or later we will suffer. We have to establish boundaries to try to protect ourselves, but we also have to realize that if we are dealing with difficult people, they will always violate those boundaries.

At the same time, loving these people does not always mean that we have to smile and put up with their ways. Sometimes love means saying, "No, this is unacceptable." That might mean that they lash out at us. In that case, our suffering will be to bear the brunt of their anger and to accept the fact that it may take time for them to realize that we really mean them well. Sometimes love even means taking the risk that they will never talk to us again, but we love them so much that we are willing to take that risk.

COMPASSION FOR THOSE WHO HURT US

Ideally, we should even have compassion on those that hurt us. When others hurt us, we should feel badly for them and, recognizing how broken they are, we would hurt for them.

We certainly see this in Jesus' death on the cross. Jesus asks the Father to forgive the very people who are crucifying him. He is more concerned about them than about himself. It would be as if someone were to slap you across the face, and your response would be, "Did you hurt your hand?"

We see this again in the third Eucharistic Prayer. We hear that Jesus gave us the gift of the Eucharist on the very night that he was betrayed. Normally, when one is betrayed, one responds with anger, frustration, and hurt. Jesus did not do that. He responded to his being betrayed by saying to himself, "Those poor people. They don't know what they are doing. I know what I'll do! I'll show them more of my love."

This, of course, requires enormous amounts of introspection and prayer. It is so easy to slip into the world's way of dealing with difficult situations. But we are Christians; we are called to be Christlike. We have to destroy the power of hurt through love. St. Maximilian Kolbe, who was sent to the Nazi concentration camp in Auschwitz, was asked by a fellow prisoner, "Shouldn't we hate the Nazis?" He answered, "No, for only love conquers."

Furthermore, at a personal level, responding in love to those who hurt us can have an enormous impact on the world. There is so much suffering, so much pain in the world. We can feel overwhelmed and helpless to change it. Yet, if we choose to love one person who is truly broken, then we have begun to transform the earth.

CHAPTER 5

EMBRACING SUFFERING IN OUR LIVES

We've seen how Jesus responds to suffering. So what do we, as Christians, do with suffering in our lives? How can we embrace suffering and use it for our good? How can we respond in a way that is like Christ?

There are no simple answers, since each person experiences suffering in a different way. However, the suggestions offered here may be helpful. Even if you find some of these ideas challenging at times, keep them in mind and use them as a goal. They don't make our suffering go away, but they can help us to find meaning in our pain and enable us to use our experiences to grow closer to God.

TRANSFORMATIVE SUFFERING

Just as Jesus transformed the cross into an instrument of salvation, the suggestions that follow can help to transform a terrible situation into a moment of grace. These are only a few of the possible strategies for dealing with suffering. It may not be possible to use all of them all of the time, but maybe we can use some of them when they are appropriate and when we have the grace and the strength to embrace them.

Trust in the Midst of Suffering

As discussed in the previous chapter, we can try to trust in the midst of suffering. Every suffering situation is an invitation. It is always possible to say no to an invitation. We can always become angry and bitter; that is clear. But suffering is an opportunity to learn to trust at a level that we may never have experienced before. This does not mean that we have to like what is happening, but it is a chance to surrender our lives and our hearts to God's love.

Embrace the Cross with a Sense of Dignity

People watch us. They can see how we respond to the difficulties in our lives. They can see whether our faith consists just words or is a profoundly lived reality.

When we carry our crosses with a spirit of hope and dignity, firmly believing that the reality we are living has a deeper dimension, then we give witness to something that goes beyond words. Our attitude fills people with a sense of awe and wonder. It makes them think that they can choose another way to deal with suffering, and it may even help them to trust in the midst of their own difficulties.

Develop a Sense of Gratitude

Our ultimate goal when we suffer is to develop a sense of gratitude for what we are experiencing. This is far more than putting up with suffering or even surrendering to it. Gratitude means that we are thankful for what we are experiencing (or more often, for what we have already experienced). We realize that it has made us the people we are now. We do not have to appreciate it in the sense of liking it. In fact, if we were given the choice of experiencing it or not, we would probably try to avoid it. But even so, we recognize that something very good has happened in our hearts. If we had not gone through the suffering, then we might never have come to our present level of insight and wisdom.

It often takes quite a bit of time before we feel this gratitude. In fact, it might take the rest of our lives. If we don't yet feel very grateful, this does not mean that we are doing anything wrong, only that it is very difficult.

Offer Up Our Suffering

Life is filled with suffering. When we can't avoid it, we still have a choice. We can put up with it and get through it, or we can make it meaningful by offering it up. One of the worst things about suffering, in fact, is when it seems to be meaningless and pointless.

But what does "offering it up" mean? Again, think of that level of communication that goes beyond words. We could say to God, "If I have to suffer, then I would like to suffer with love. If in any way my suffering can lighten the burden of this person or that situation, then let me carry my cross with love." Suffering, which usually makes us feel all alone and abandoned, thus becomes a way to reach out in a profound way to others who are suffering. Furthermore, in offering up our sufferings we are not giving in to the tendency to play the victim. It is so easy to say, "Woe is me! This is the worst thing that could ever happen!" Sometimes, this is even true, but when we offer it up, suffering becomes an opportunity to be generous and altruistic.

Even if others are not suffering, we still might want to offer up our pain as an act of love that could edify and spiritually challenge others (whether they know that we are doing this or not). When we are surrounded by good, loving people who are willing to offer up their suffering for us, it can have a powerful effect on us.

We all make mistakes in life. We all regret hurting people by the things we did or didn't do. Of course, it's too late to change things once they've happened. Yet offering up our suffering for someone we have hurt in the past could be a way of offering them our love. This could be the beginning of their healing from the wounds that we have caused them. In fact, this could be a much more profound way of expressing our love than words ever could be. (Not that we shouldn't use words, but they can sound easy and cheap if they are not backed up with actions.)

We may never actually know how much healing has occurred. Yet, when people are loved, it always changes their reality. We know that children cannot thrive physically if they are not hugged and caressed. Offering up our pain and suffering for someone is a spiritual hug that will begin a process of healing. (In a similar manner, prayer is also a way of reaching out, for in prayer our love is united with God's love and we embrace the people for whom we have prayed.)

We can also offer up our suffering for others so that it might lead them to conversion. We are frustrated by the bad choices that people whom we love sometimes make. We don't know how to "bring them around." This is one way. Furthermore, conversion is always a bit painful. We are creatures of habit (even if they are bad habits). By offering up our suffering for the people who need to change their ways, we are taking on a bit of their pain, the pain they would suffer in giving up their old, familiar ways for new, more loving patterns of behavior.

We can work on our own conversion in the same manner. We can try to give up a bad habit, offering up the discomfort of making this change for someone who needs our love. We might promise to drink less, pray more, eat more carefully, exercise more. What is significant is that these decisions will not be made as acts of discipline, but rather as acts of love, which often enables us to succeed. This is especially important for those of us who make all sorts of resolutions that don't seem to last. The irony is that we will only be doing what we should have been doing all along, but now, instead of it being an act of will, it is an offering of love.

Identify with the Suffering of Others

One of the effects of suffering is that it isolates us. We wonder if others could possibly understand what we're going through or even if they care.

And yet one of the effects of suffering is exactly the opposite: it actually helps us understand better what others are going through. It becomes a motivation to reach out to them, either directly or spiritually. We are not the only ones who are depressed or suffering from mental illness. We are not the only ones who are childless or widowed or unable to find a special someone. We are not the only ones with heart disease or cancer or AIDS. We are not alone, and neither are the others who are suffering in the same way we are. We form a bond of compassion through the very thing we hate the most.

Forgive as a Response to the Suffering of Betrayal

When we have experienced the suffering of betrayal, it can take a long, long time for us to trust again. We tend to go through a series of confused emotions, and it is important not to short-circuit that process. At the same time, sooner or later we have to let go of the hurt and forgive. As long as we hold on to the resentment, it continues to be a festering sore in our souls. Forgiving the other person is not based on the fact that the other person deserves it or has even asked for it. Forgiveness is based on the recognition that the other person is broken and needs our love. We might have to love that person from a distance. Some people are toxic, and there are some moments in our lives when we are so emotionally fragile that we cannot deal with that person. But we still pray for that person, and more than anything we feel compassion when we realize how many problems that person has.

THE BLESSINGS OF SUFFERING

As noted previously, one of the most frustrating aspects of suffering is that it often seems to be meaningless. We put up with it, but our only goal is to get through it. Might there be ways that we can make it more meaningful? Could it, in fact, be a form of blessing? Here are some suggestions as to how we can transform something that we often consider a curse into an opportunity to grow in love.

Suffering Can Be an Opportunity to Love

Even if we don't understand why suffering occurs, we can still use it as an opportunity to reach out to others. Whether it be a family member or a friend or even someone living on the other side of the planet, we can offer to help them in their need. We can offer financial help when there is a natural disaster or even volunteer to travel to places that have been affected. We can bring casseroles to those who have lost a loved one or to a family that is going through some type of crisis. We can visit the sick or those in nursing homes or those who are in prison. We can just ask people, "How are you doing?" and then wait for the answer.

If we reach out to others, it might mean that we don't have the time or energy to do everything that we wanted to do. If we take care of a sick relative, it will limit our freedom. If we visit someone with Alzheimer's disease, then we will have to deal with their confusion and our feelings of loss. We will have to sit there, not even knowing if the other person recognizes who we are. If we visit a hospital, we may feel uncomfortable with the situation or the smells and sights we encounter. This is sacrificial love, the love that Christ has for us.

Suffering Can Strengthen Us

If we intend to live as Christians, then we are going to have to pay a price. We probably won't be arrested by the secret police and put on trial for our faith. But we may be misunderstood and taken advantage of. We may be accused of being a fool or old-fashioned. We may be asked why we are going to church again. We will not be able to do certain things that others do—not that they should be doing those things!

In the early church, Christians often felt privileged to be able to suffer for the faith. This should be our attitude. If we respond to torments with defensiveness and anger, if we become self-righteous and feel superior to others, what does that say about our interior disposition? But if we quietly and joyfully undergo these tests, doesn't it show that our faith is pure and authentic?

Suffering Can Give Us a New Perspective on Life

It seems that in times of suffering, we learn what's really important. In normal times, we go through life seeking to live well and peacefully, but we can often get caught up with things that, when you come right down to it, are not important. We even can get into a rut in which we bicker over insignificant "problems" that are often little more than annoyances.

When we bring a loved one to the emergency room, when we are standing by the bed of a child who might not make it, when we receive the diagnosis that we have cancer, then we quickly reevaluate what is going on, and we realize that some things are significant while others are not.

Of course, we have to be careful, since suffering can cause its own series of distractions. We may find ourselves exhausted and short-tempered. Our anger may flare up irrationally against the very people whom we love the most. As long as we recognize the pull in that direction, we can short-circuit the painful emotions before we do or say things that we will later regret.

Suffering Can Purify Us

When we sin, we bring a brokenness into our lives. God forgives us, but we often hold on to the brokenness. It is easier for us to choose what is wrong. It is easier for us to act in a selfish manner.

Every act of goodness here on earth helps to heal that brokenness. This is why we have a penance during the Sacrament of Reconciliation. Penance is not paying the fine for our sins. It is an act of goodness that begins the process of healing what we have wounded through our sins.

What hasn't been fully healed here on earth will have to be healed in purgatory. In purgatory, we want to be with Christ, but the residue of selfishness in our hearts keeps us from fully surrendering to that love. Purgatory is not a punishment; it's a purification. Christ's love gives us the courage to let go of whatever is still unhealed and to trust completely in his love.

Can suffering bring purification? We often hear of people who have suffered horribly before they died. People say that they must have gone right to heaven because they already had their purgatory here on earth. Is that true? Suffering in itself does not make someone better. When we choose to trust in God and when we offer up our suffering as an act of love for others, then we certainly do heal our brokenness. When we become nasty and resentful and miserable, then we do not really grow through that suffering. It is not the suffering itself that makes us grow, but our response to the suffering.

There is an old saying that we can't accomplish anything worthwhile without a certain amount of suffering. When we suffer for doing something good or noble, is Satan trying to hinder our work, or is God giving us an opportunity to sort out any improper motivations so that we can do our task in the right spirit? It is not always clear. Yet if we are certain in the Spirit that what we are doing is from God, then a period of purification helps filter out those improper motivations, such as pride. If we are uncertain, however, then we must discern whether the difficulties we are encountering are a sign from God to slow down and rethink our mission, lest we try to do that which is not God's will.

Suffering Can Help Us Accept Our Limitations

We often go through life thinking that we are invulnerable. Suffering reminds us that we will not live forever. Time is precious, and every minute should be used as if it were our last. It also teaches us that we cannot do everything. No matter how much we resent it, there are limitations to what we can do. As we grow older, our energy levels are not what they once were. We feel the aches and pains of everyday life. We suffer from a diminishment of the senses. It is good to set realistic goals for ourselves and to be aware that there is only so much we can do. This is true at any age of our lives, for we often seek to do it all, and that can leave us exhausted and resentful. Suffering can remind us to say no once in a while.

Suffering Can Help Us Learn to Ask for Help

One of the important lessons that we can learn through suffering is to reach out and ask for help from others. Most of us expend great energy trying to be and remain autonomous. We do not really like to depend on others. After all, they might not be available. They might ask for something in return. We would have to admit we can't do it alone. Most of us would much rather offer someone else assistance than ask for help.

Yet, when we suffer, we come to realize that we really can't make it on our own. We might need physical help, like assistance getting out of bed. We might need psychological help; perhaps we need someone who can listen to our fears and confusion. But in order to ask for help, we have to be willing to become vulnerable.

There are two moments in Jesus' life when he is most clearly vulnerable: his birth and his death. He became a little, helpless child and asked us to care for him. In his death, he placed himself in our hands, trusting in us even when he knew that we didn't deserve that trust. He could have called upon the angels to protect him. Instead, he became vulnerable to teach us that love involves not only serving others, but also letting ourselves be served.

When we don't ask for help in those times when we really need it, we are not only being arrogantly self-sufficient, we are also robbing from others the opportunity to act charitably. When we ask for help, we are giving others the possibility of expressing their love by serving us. Thus, asking for help is not a defeat; it is a ministry. There comes a point in our lives, in fact, when our primary ministry to the community will be to ask for help.

A Few Caveats

Should We Ask for Suffering?

If suffering can have all of this spiritual value, should we seek it? We might apply the lesson that St. Margaret of Cortona offered when she was asked whether Christians should seek out new forms of poverty. Her answer was, "No! There is enough of it already to go around." Most of us already have enough suffering in our lives.

Jesus, after all, did not pray in the Garden of Gethsemane, "Bring it on!" Rather, he said, "Anything but this, but if this is what you want, then your will be done." When we are suffering, we don't have to want to continue to suffer. We should seek relief. If we have a choice between sitting on a beach or being caught in a blizzard, we should choose the beach. When we are ill, we should seek to alleviate our pain. We should go to the doctor, to the counselor, to the healing services in our churches. We should pray for healing from our Lord. But if after all of that, we are still suffering, we should try to surrender and find peace.

What if We Suffer Poorly?

Nobody suffers perfectly. We would all like to bear with suffering like the great saints. The only problem is that even the great saints sometimes had their difficulties. Suffering intensely before she died, St. Thérèse of Lisieux was tempted to commit suicide. We tend to hear about the saints' successes, but even they struggled.

Sometimes no matter how much we want to be courageous, it just doesn't happen. Sometimes the fear takes over, and we find it difficult to trust. And sometimes we feel so discouraged that we just want it to end.

This is a part of our surrender: that no one does it perfectly. We have to do all that we can and trust that God will supply what we can't. We shouldn't beat ourselves up for what we can't do.

Can We Be Crushed by Our Suffering?

And what if one is crushed by suffering? We would like to believe that God would not send a burden too heavy for us to carry.

The difficulty of that saying is that if we are crushed, then we not only feel crushed but also guilty for allowing it to happen. We have to ask ourselves what this saying means. If God's perspective is for the long run, then perhaps what happens in the short term is part of God's larger plan. If I have a nervous breakdown, maybe it will teach me to reach out for help, and it will give my family an opportunity to serve me. If I become furious at God, maybe it will force me to reexamine what I really expect from him and whether that coincides with what God has actually promised. If I can't take it any longer and pray to die, maybe it is God's way of helping me to loosen my grip on this world so that I'll be ready to go to the next. There are situations that are so painful and traumatic and confusing that they can overwhelm us, but sometimes in "losing," we learn a new way of "winning."

So would God send a situation too painful for us to bear? It depends on what we mean by not being able to bear it. Remember, if we lose with love, then we still win.

CHAPTER 6

BACK TO THE BEGINNING: DOES GOD SEND SUFFERING?

We've come back to a question that we asked at the beginning: would a loving God cause the suffering of his beloved children? We are not just talking about God allowing suffering to occur; we are talking about whether God actually sends suffering into people's lives. This idea is such a distasteful one that many of us naturally reject it. We often hear that God is good and loving and therefore wouldn't torture people. But what does salvation history teach us?

Old Testament authors firmly believed that God was the source of all things, good and bad. Remember, Job said that if we thank God in good times, we should also thank him in bad times. They also speak often of God sending bad things into the lives of his people when they have sinned. He punished them. One could argue that the punishment was God just stepping back and letting his people experience the consequences of their sins. But other passages are more proactive, stating that it was God who sent the thunderbolts and locusts and Assyrian troops. Yet, even in the most pessimistic catalogue of punishments, we hear a bit of hope: God would restore a remnant; God did not hate his people; God wanted to purify them.

Furthermore, we begin to hear of God bringing forgiveness to his people through the suffering of a mysterious figure called the Suffering Servant of Yahweh. The Jewish people did not really believe that anyone's suffering could bring forgiveness of sins, but that is exactly what we find in the four poems of the Suffering Servant in the book of the prophet Isaiah (chapter 53). Jesus later applied these poems to himself, using them to describe his own mission (Matthew 12:17-21).

The Messiness of Creation

Long before humans came into this world, it was a messy place. Dinosaurs killed one another, earthquakes and tidal waves caused destruction, and viruses and bacteria caused diseases. There is no question that sin multiplied suffering, but even before we arrived, there was a lot of suffering occurring in the world.

Some people might object that this is positing that God created a world in which bad existed. It would be useful to distinguish here between bad and evil. Bad means that things are messy and harmful; evil, on the other hand, refers to things that are morally wrong. It is bad to break a toe, but not necessarily evil. It is bad for the lion to eat the gazelle (at least for the gazelle), but not evil. God created everything good. We hear this phrase multiple times in Genesis (1:4, 1:10, 1:12, 1:18, 1:21, 1:25, 1:31). God created the best of all worlds—morally, but not in terms of natural perfection. This means that God created a world in which messy things happen but in which all things reflect the glory of God.

GOD AND FREE WILL

Could we blame the messiness and suffering on the freedom that God gave to humanity and the world in creation? We know that God has given us free will. Some theologians speak of how God also gave a degree of freedom to the created world. They would argue that God does not decide every little thing. God got the ball rolling, and now it rolls on its own.

In this view, suffering is not a punishment, nor does God have anything to do with it. It just happens. When someone has a heart attack, there is no one to blame. It is just the way things are.

We do hear an echo of this idea in certain passages in the Bible. In Psalm 14:1, we read, "Fools say in their hearts, 'There is no God.'" The psalmist is not really speaking about atheists.

He is speaking about people who believe that God exists but just doesn't care about us. God is so transcendent that he does not get involved in our everyday lives.

At the time of Jesus, there was a group of Jews called the Sadducees who took this view. They emphasized the transcendence of God and deemphasized how much God was involved in their lives. They did not believe in angels, as the Pharisees did, nor did they believe in messengers from God. They did not even believe that God had a plan for their lives.

There is a value to this position as a corrective to those who would posit too much divine involvement. Does God send every squirrel that walks across our front yard? Does God prefer that we wear a blue sweater today or a red one? If God is that involved, then there is no true freedom. Everything is determined, and we are only puppets being moved by a divine puppet master.

Yet, it would also be a mistake to argue the opposite—that God is not involved in what happens. If he were not involved, how could we thank him for the good things in life? But how much of what happens is God's will, and how much is caused by our free will? The best way to answer this question is to say that God has a plan, and we have a plan, and there is a partnership between God and us. In any good partnership, it is difficult to determine who is making the final decision. People who have been married for a long time even finish each other's sentences because they know exactly what the other is thinking. That is like God and us. Sometimes God is more in charge, sometimes we are.

Of course, God is evidently the senior partner, and even if we are "in charge," it is only because God has allowed it. But God is always somehow in the mix. Even if I bring some of my suffering on myself by what I eat or drink or by taking other unnecessary risks, God at the very least allows me to suffer the consequences of what I have done. But it also seems as if God is sometimes more involved than that, and might actually cause some of the bad things to occur.

GOD'S WAY OF HELPING US TO GROW

Might God allow or send some suffering into our lives so that we can feel the consequences of our sins and perhaps turn away from sin? Any parent who truly loves a child must be willing to punish that child if that is what is truly needed. Some parents are afraid that the punishment would cause the child to be angry with them. But if the parents worry too much about this outcome, then it means that they are more concerned with their own good than that of the child. God is not worried about himself. He will do whatever he can to bring us around.

We could also ask whether a loving parent might allow a child to face a challenge if the parent knew that this would help the child grow. It pains the parent to see the child struggle, but the parent is willing to carry some pain for the sake of the child, which is the pain of having to stand by and let the child go through the difficulty. If life is too easy for the child, then that child could easily become egocentric, thinking that the world revolves around him or her. Could God allow us to suffer so that we could grow up and learn the difference between what is important and what is not? Would a loving parent do that?

Besides, God sees the long term results while we are so often caught up in the short term. We see the immediate suffering, while God sees the widening of the limits of our hearts and the compassion we learn and the empathy we express toward each other. God sees how we learn to reevaluate life with his perspective and how we learn to put aside our selfish and sometimes childish points of view. Thus, might God allow or cause suffering to help make us better people?

Of course, we could always turn down that invitation to grow. We could decide to allow suffering to make us bitter and cynical. God can't force us to love; he can only invite us. Suffering might be one of the ways he invites us to love him and others in a deeper way.

GOD'S WAYS ARE NOT OUR WAYS

Finally, even after we try to reason this all out, we have to recognize that God's reasoning is so far beyond what we can understand that we can only capture a glimpse of it. God's ways are not like our ways. We cannot say God would or would not do this or that simply because it doesn't make sense to us. The Father sent his Son into the world to take our sins and suffering upon himself in his death on the cross. Jesus interpreted his mission from the Father in terms of suffering and dying for us. Yahweh, the loving Father, called his Son to the cross.

Jesus further adds that if we want to be his followers, then we will have to take up our own crosses and follow him (Matthew 16:24). Our suffering, in fact, is identified as an opportunity to make up what is lacking in the sufferings of Christ (Colossians 1:24). God's wisdom, the wisdom of the cross which is a stumbling block to Jews and foolishness to Gentiles, is more profound than the wisdom of the world. God created in his image and likeness. We reflect that image and likeness when we follow the example of Christ, who lived and died for us.

Many of the saints over the centuries certainly felt that a loving God had sent suffering into their lives as a sign of his love. We need only to think of St. Francis of Assisi and St. Padre Pio, both of whom received the stigmata and grew in love because of it. Could a loving God send suffering into our lives to call us back from horrible mistakes, or even to invite us to a greater love?

WHY DO THE INNOCENT SUFFER?

Still, here is always that lingering question: why do the innocent suffer? In Fyodor Dostoevsky's novel *The Brothers Karamazov*, one of the characters states that if even one innocent child suffers in the world, then he cannot believe in a good God. We can spiritualize our own sufferings, but what about infants?

Certainly, their plight can be a motivation for us to reach out and help them. But would God allow them to suffer just so that we can do good deeds?

Innocent suffering also promotes a generosity of another sort. How many parents have said, "I wish it were me going through this rather than my child." Such a situation can even promote guilt. A parent will ask, "What did I do that God is punishing my child?" We assume that there must be some clear cause, and we blame ourselves. Yet, would a loving God be so vindictive as to punish a small child for a parent's fault? Remember, the prophet Ezekiel warned that we should no longer say that the fathers ate sour grapes and that the children's teeth were set on edge (18:2). Each person is responsible for his or her own guilt.

The birth of Jesus is actually tied to this phenomenon. We can speak of the privations of the holy family. Or even more poignantly, we can speak of the suffering of the holy innocents, those children who were killed by King Herod's troops in his paranoid attempt to kill the newborn king of the Jews (see Matthew 2:16-18). The church speaks of them giving silent witness to the birth of the King of kings.

THEOLOGICAL MYSTERIES DON'T GET SOLVED

Ultimately, we don't have an answer. This is the messiest part of suffering. If we were in charge, we would probably think that this is the first thing we would address. We would like to wrestle God on this one, and Job does exactly that in his arguments with God, but eventually we will walk away limping. The suffering of the innocent can leave us wondering if we can even trust God, but somehow we do (although there is always a bittersweet aspect to that trust, much like Abraham must have felt after offering to sacrifice his only beloved son to God).

We have to leave the question here, for this might be as far as we can go. We are, after all, dealing with a mystery, and theological mysteries don't get solved. Does suffering happen? Does God allow it? Does God cause it? Is it the consequence of our bad choices? Is it the consequence of sin? Maybe all of these are true on some level.

So the question then becomes, how do we respond to the mystery? We hold onto God for dear life. We try to be honest and trusting. We surrender our lives and our love into God's loving arms.

Heaven, the Mystery of Love

When we reflect upon suffering, one of our greatest consolations is that we know it will not last forever. Even Job believed that there would be an end to it. Unfortunately, for him, he believed that the end marked the end of all things, for he could only look forward to that shadowy existence of Sheol.

We, on the other hand, believe that a heaven awaits us in which there are no tears. There will be no harm on God's holy mountain. The lion will lie down with the lamb (see Isaiah 65:25). But what will this mean?

Many of us have an image of heaven that makes it seem like a type of spiritual Disneyland. There will be angels with ostrich feather fans to cool us, and other angels will peel grapes to drop into our open mouths. Every non-sinful desire will be satisfied. The joys of heaven will more than make up for any misery that we have suffered upon the earth.

When you think about it, however, this image of heaven is a bit selfish. It is almost as if we are saying, "I'll put up with eighty years of misery as long as I get an eternity of pleasure." Something is wrong with this idea, for when we get to heaven, we are supposed to be like God. When God was born upon this earth, he was not selfish. He served others.

God, in the person of Jesus, teaches us that to be Godlike, we must love and serve and heal others. At the Last Supper, Jesus said he knew where he was from and where he was going, and so he washed the disciples' feet (see John 13). This was not an act of humiliation that denied who Jesus was; it was the revelation of what it meant to be like God.

Likewise, the cross is not called the hour of shame in the Gospel of John; instead, it is called the hour of glory. Remember, the word "glory" is redefined in this gospel. It is not the revelation of power or magnificence; it is the outpouring of love. The cross is where we see that love most clearly.

We aspire to the glory of heaven, but many of us still interpret that idea as receiving honor and privilege. We even ask who will get a better seat in heaven. The glory of heaven, however, is not about prestige. It is about that same outpouring of love that we see upon the cross. There is something about the cross that makes it the most profound revelation of what heaven will be like. There will be no physical suffering there, but there will be an outpouring of love.

And so the mystery of suffering is not just for this world, as if this were a torture chamber from which we graduate at the end of our lives into a more blessed existence. Rather, there is something in the mystery that reveals the essence of what will come. It speaks of surrender and trust. It calls us to be less self-centered. It hints at things that we just cannot understand now, but that will become clear when we see God face-to-face.

This might explain why Jesus tells us that the road to heaven is narrow and difficult. It is difficult to embrace our crosses here on earth, and it will also be difficult to say yes to God's love for all eternity. Of course, the more we do it on earth, the less difficult it will be then. But if we have the courage to reach out and embrace our crosses and say, "Not my will but your will be done," then we will have entered into a great mystery of love.